TABLE

"THE SILVER IS MINE, AND THE GOLD IS MINE, SAITH THE LORD OF HOSTS." HAGGAI 2:8

INTRODUCTION

Money which is an integral part of wealth is a very important aspect to our living. The Bible said that money answers all things. With money we can live a life of comfort, buy whatever with desire in life to keep us moving. For example, with money we can buy food, cars, house, marry, raise our children, travel for vacation, pay medical bills, pay our bills, give out to charity, support missions, help in expanding the work of God, and many more things we can do with money. So let us not allow the devil to deceive us through ignorance that having money on this earth is a bad thing.

Say with me now! "The devil you are a liar and you will continue to be a liar."

Dictionary.com defines wealth as

1. A great quantity or store of money, valuable possession, property, or other riches: the wealth of a city.

2. An abundance or profusion of anything, or plentiful.

It will also be good to know that the synonyms of wealth are affluence, prosperity, riches, means, substance, fortune, cash, money, lucre, capital, treasure, finance, and many more.

This book, **the Bible of Prosperity** will help us to understand that being wealthy in biblical concept is a divine and covenant wealth; it will also help us to understand our rightful place as children of God when it comes to being wealthy. This book of books will also address the misconceptions about being rich in possessions

Finally this book of books will enrich you with the simple steps to turning your dreams into reality which will in turn empower you to move forward to acquire massive possessions of material and

spiritual wealth for yourself, for your family,

for charity, and ultimately for the expansion

of the work of God.

Chapter one

ACKWOLEDGE GOD AS YOUR FATHER

For you to acquire divine wealth you need to believe in God as the source to every lasting wealth which comes with peace of mind. Deuteronomy 8:18 says that, "But thou shalt remember the Lord thy God: for it is He that gives thee power to get wealth, that He may establish His covenant which He swore unto thy fathers, as it is this day." Therefore as a Christian you are entitled by the grace of God to inherit covenant wealth, which is wealth without working for it. It is

the gift and the promise from God.

And also have it in the back of your

mind that there is a spiritual Garden of Eden

where Jesus Christ is in charge. He was that

tree of life in the physical Garden of Eden

which the first earthly Adam failed to eat

and rather ate the tree of good and evil. So

that tree of life which is Jesus Christ came in

the flesh, and paid a price by shedding His

precious blood in the cross of Calvary that

you, and I should be able enter into the

spiritual Garden of Eden with all boldness in

time of need. The Bible said in **Hebrews 10:14-20,**

(14) For by one offering He hath perfected forever them that are sanctified.

(15) Whereof the Holy Ghost also is a witness to us: for that He had said before, (16) this is the covenant that I will make with them after those days, said the Lord, I will put my laws into their hearts, and in their minds will I write them; (17) And their sins and iniquities will I remember no more.

(18) Now where remission of these is, there is no more offering for sin. (19) Having therefore, brethren, boldness to enter into the holiest by the blood of Jesus, (20) by a new living way which he hath consecrated for us, through the veil, that is to say, His flesh.

2 Corinthians 8:9 also put a clearer picture to what it meant by inheriting covenant wealth it says;

"For ye know the grace of our Lord Jesus Christ, that though He was rich, yet for your sakes He became poor, that ye through His poverty might be rich."

Friends! I bet the principles found in this book works, you just got to sincere believe every word in this book, and I assure you that you achieve your desire goals at ease.

How the Spiritual Garden of Eden works

Saint John's gospel chapter 15, helps us to understand the leadership hierarchy in the Spiritual Garden of Eden which is the foundation to acquiring massive wealth, it

says that Jesus Christ is the true vine, while
God our Father is the husbandman, and that
we are the branches. Jesus Christ
expectation for us is to be **fruitful** that is
why He came to this world and shed His
blood at the cross of Calvary.

He went further to elaborate that Jesus
is the vine, and we are the branches, and that
if we abide in Him, and He in us, then we
shall bear **much fruit,** for without Him we
can do nothing.

Then what is Fruit?

Fruit here means abundance of wealth, increase in all things, possessions, greatness, healing, joy, abundant and many more. We get to understand that being fruitful is a gift from God, and we are not required to work for it. Therefore enjoying the goodness of God is a special grace handed to us by God which is our Father and creator.

The way it works in the Spiritual is this, we are the branches attacked to the vine which is our Lord Jesus Christ, in Him all the nutrients in which the tree needs to survive and bear fruit is

complete. His precious blood cleanses the tree, the root and the branches.

The Spiritual soil is heaven the throne of God while the

Husbandman is the almighty God, our Father, and our Creator.

The emphases here is that the Almighty God is **our Father,** therefore it is our birthright to be wealthy, to be rich, be excellent in all things, be the head, be powerful, be creative, be intelligent, have enough, be smart and many more.

The Important of the Lord's Prayer

Jesus Christ taught His disciples on how to pray He said, **"Our Father who art in heaven, thy Kingdom come as it is in heaven……"** Here He wanted His disciples to know that God is there Father, and that He takes them as His children, He also wanted them to understand that God's intention is for His children is to have the same luxury as they have in heaven.

Apostle Peter had an opportunity to

ask Jesus Christ a life time question

which will be very vital as long as

Christianity exist. He asked, "……,

Behold we have forsaken all, and

followed thee; what shall we have

therefore?" Jesus Christ answered in

Matthew 19: 28-29

**"Verily I say unto you, that
ye which have followed me, in the
regeneration when the son of man
shall sit in the throne of His glory,
ye also shall sit upon twelve
thrones, judging the twelve tribes of
Israel.**

And every one that hath forsaken houses, or brethren, or sisters, or father, or mother, or wife, or children, or lands, for my name's sake, shall receive a hundredfold, and shall inherit everlasting life."

It is very important for you to understand that in heaven there is no lack, no pains, no hatred, no sickness, no death, no debt, no poverty, no sadness, and no wars etc. The Bible said that in heaven its city is paved with gold, Jesus Christ is the Morning

Star who produces constant light or electricity. The Angels are the servants of the **Most High God**, which we can say they are the cooks, and the drivers of the Will of God. As children of God the Angels are our servant because the Spirit that is in God and in Jesus Christ abides in us. **John 15: 15-16** said that,

Jesus Christ said to His disciples (you and I):

Henceforth I call you not servants; for the servant knows not what his lord

doeth: but I have called you

friends, for all things that I

have heard of my Father I

have made known to you (15).

Ye have not chosen me,

but I have chosen you, and

ordained you, that ye should

go and bring forth fruit, and

that your fruit should

remain: that whatsoever ye

shall ask of the Father in my

name, ye may give it you (16).

Jesus Christ here was initiating the

Kingdom principle to His disciples; He

wanted them to understand that fruitfulness is the major part of the Kingdom of God. He also wanted them to know that they are ordained for success, for increase, for plenty, for wealth, for breakthrough and all you can name of.

He was also trying to convince His disciples that the same way God looks at the saints in heaven is the same way God looks at them. God sees all of us as His children and has given us everything that pertains to live and godliness, we don't need to work for it because Jesus Christ paid the price at the cross of Calvary by shedding His precious blood for us to enjoy the good of this earth. The Bible also said that **Jesus Christ became poor that we might be rich.** In **John 10:10** Jesus Christ that,

"The thief cometh not, but for to steal, and to destroy: I am come that they might have life, and that they might have it more abundantly." Jesus Christ is telling us here that He came to this earth to give us abundant life which is a life filled with purpose, prosperity, good health, and comfort, plenty of spiritual and massive material wealth, possessions and whatever good things you can think of.

If you really want to be massively wealthy on this earth and live a peaceful life from God you just get to believe that God is your **Father and meant what he promise you as stated in the Bible and He can bring it to pass today;** hear what He said in Isaiah 49:15-16;

Can a woman forget her sucking child, that she should not have compassion on the son of her womb? Yea, they may forget, yet will I not forget thee (15).

Behold, I have graven thee upon the palms of my hands; thy walls are continually before me (16).

God wants us to understand here that He is our Father who always has us in heart because He is the one who created us, and that His thought for us is good. He wants us to act and behave as sons and daughters of God. For example, **imagine** the son of the president of a country or a business corporation, how will he act? The answer to this question is **boldness, confidence, assurance, hope, always with money; dress well, always with bodyguards, good**

health care, leave in white house, good and prominent friends, invitations to honorable party, good vacations and most all quick access to his father.

Quick access to the father is one of the privileges of a Child, here he doesn't need to make any appointment to see his father, and he goes in and out at his will. He is free to go to the kitchen and eat whatever he wants. He can request from the father one of his clothing. In summary the son have every privilege and right of to the President. Unlike the son of a President, we are the children of the Most High God, therefore

God want us to come to Him with that boldness as His children with all the full right believing that Jesus Christ was sent by Him to come and bring us back to Him. That wall, barrier, partition that separated us from God has been nullified through the blood of Christ. The Bible says **that there is live in the blood,** that means blood speaks, blood has body parts, it can walk, can breathe, has ears, can travel and can give life.

Think of this, our God is a God of prosperity, wealth, and of luxury, so He wants us to live that way, have enough to be a blessing to them who don't have. He wants us to keep on asking Him for more good things. **The book of psalms wrote that God will increase our greatness and comfort us by every side.** Psalmist also made us to understand that God seated in heaven and does all that pleases Him. He loves us when we ask Him for things that look impossible in the eyes of men. The Bibles said that **"for with God nothing shall be impossible."** Then why not ask Him for great ideas, massive possessions, great wealth, beautiful wife, good friends, money, good home, good children, good cars and most of all good spiritual way of living. The book of **James 1:5-7 says**;

If any of you lack wisdom, let him ask of God, that gives to all men liberally, and upbraided not; and it shall be given him (5).

But let him ask in faith nothing wavering. For he that wavered is like a wave of the sea driven with the wind and tossed (6).

For let not that man think that he shall receive any thing of the Lord (7).

Apostle James Massive Wealth Wisdom Strategies

1. **Wisdom to make wealth:** James encourages us to ask God for wisdom because this is the gateway to prosperity. For example, Solomon the riches man on this planet earth being known was a man full of wisdom form God and the Bible confirms that he was prosperous. Some time ago a Pastor friend of mine said to me, "Emmanuel only what you need to succeed in this world is for you to ask God for an idea," at this point of time I was just a young Evangelist going about preaching the word of God by hosting crusades, and seminars. I

would like to tell you today his simple counsel have blessed my life, and ministry, souls have been restored for the Kingdom of God. I also will be bold to tell you that God in heaven have supply all my needs according to His riches in glory through Christ Jesus.

What I did was to kneel down in humility and ask God for His wisdom concerning His calling upon my life. He answered my prayer. So what you need is to spend a little time to ask for His wisdom on how to acquire massive wealth for the sole purpose of

being a blessing to humanity and the

things of God. It will be very

important to remind you that the **Holy**

Bible is the greatest, the most

valuable book in this world, and even

in the spiritual world because it is

God Himself. Whatever it says has

power to fulfil its purposes. This

Book is the Ancient book of Ages that

has never lie, and is always ready to

transform lives and situation. The

Bible said asks for wisdom, therefore

never be afraid to ask for the wisdom

from God for massive wealth because it is your birthright.

2. **Ask in faith:** Faith here means asking for the wisdom of massive wealth and believing that you have received it. Believing means you start acting, thinking, dress, position yourself as if it is already in your possession knowing you will have as a child of God.

3. **God:** Always acknowledge God in all your doings; always get connected to Him because He is the one that gives the wisdom, and the power to make wealth. Apostle James in his epistle

said "….let he asks of God that

gives to all men liberally…"

God our Father wants us to discover

who we are and then act in boldness like

a Lion to take possession of what we

want in life. He has given us all that

pertain to life freely as His children but

our fate is in our hand. Therefore we

need to change our behavior and attitude

from **mediocrity to prosperity** knowing

that it is Him that owns all, and have

giving it to us. He gets angry when we

don't prosper because He sees us still

living under ignorance which is the

bondage from the devil. God spoke to us in **Psalm 2:6-8;**

Yet have I set my king upon my Holy hill Zion (6).

I will declare the decree: the Lord hath said unto me, Thou art my son; this day have I begotten thee (7).

Ask of me, and I shall give the heathen for thine inheritance, and the uttermost parts of the earth for thy possession (8).

1. We are kings created and ordained by God

2. God calls us sons and gives us every good things as His children

3. He wants us to ask Him for that massive wealth on this earth.

I will be very bold to write in this book that if there is anyone that should be rich and wealthy in this planet earth is you and I. Study the Bible you will see that Abraham who was a friend to God was very **rich**, rich in cattle, had **lands**, had **wells**, and had **maids** and **servants.** As a friend to God and a business man he was rich, powerful to reject the gift of a king or President of a country. With his soldiers he was able to rescue his Nephew in the land of Sodom and Gomorrah.

Record also showed that Isaac the son of Abraham was also very rich. In Genesis 26, God asked Isaac to go down to Egypt and live there for He will prosper him. Isaac obeyed God and sowed in that land. The same year he received hundredfold profit from that land.

And the man (Isaac) waxed great, and went forward, and grew until he became very great (13):

For he had possession of flocks, and possession of herds, and great store of servants: and the Philistines envied him (14).

It will be very interesting to know that Isaac had **wells of water.** These great men of God are not different from us; they were created and ordained by the same God. The God that blesses them is the same God that is our Father, the same way God looks at them is the same way He looked at us. Therefore it is our right to be massively wealthy because we are the children of God, and we know better on how to make good use of His wealth for the purpose of the Kingdom of God.

As a child of God you need to see yourself as a prosperous business man, an entrepreneur, CEO of a company, a leader, a Governor, a President. Your positive imagination need to be at work which will be discussed in detail at a subsequent chapter. You just get to desire big, because that is the thought of God for you. The Bible said in Philippians 4:8,

Finally, brethren, whatsoever things are true, whatsoever things are honest, whatsoever things are

**just, whatsoever things are pure,
whatsoever things that are lovely,
whatsoever things are of good
report; if there be any virtue, and
there be any praise, think on these
things.**

Thinking of good things is the lifestyle in heaven; it is godly as long as you give all the glory to God. In heaven there is no poverty, no sickness, no tears, no pains, no disappointment, no divorce, no wars, no cheating, no jealousy, no murmuring, no killing, and no lack etc. That is why when Jesus Christ was on earth the Bible recorded that He went about doing good, healing the sick and raising the dead.

Therefore God in heaven is watching and expecting us to think of His massive blessings which are true, honest, just, pure, lovely, has a good report, has virtue and is filled with praise. He wants us to live a comfortable life on this earth as kings. He wants to connect us with men and women of wisdom. He wants us to know that He has created us with an unlimited power to make wealth in this generation; His covenant of wealth was entered with us the very day He created us into this world and exposes it to us through the Bible which is the word of God that we might not be ignorant.

God wants to understand that we are anointed for success and prosperity not just for our own consumption but to use it and help others, and also for the advancement of the kingdom of God. I will like to end this chapter by preparing you for one of the greatest adventures of the life time. All the wealthiest men in the world pass through this spiritual preparation of their mind which is known as **Preparing the Atmosphere for Wealth.**

PSALMS I

Blessed is the man that walked not in the counsel of the ungodly, nor stranded in the way of the sinners, nor sited in the seat of the scornful.

But his delight is in the law of the Lord; and in His law doth he meditate day and night (2).

And he shall be like a tree planted by the rivers of water, that brings forth his fruit in his season; his leaf also shall not wither, and whatsoever he doeth shall prosper (3).

If you really want to prosper and be wealthy, the wealth that is from God which will produce a lasting joy for you and your family. You need to read this Psalms and memorize it for your daily consumption. The Bible said in **Psalms 114:13-16;**

> **He will bless them that fear the Lord, both small and great (13).**

> **The Lord shall increase you more and more, you and your children (14).**

> **Ye are blessed of the Lord which made heaven and earth (15).**

**The heavens, even the heavens,
are the Lord's: but the earth hath
He given to the children of men
(16).**

We are the children of men in which this
scripture is talking about, so everything has
been given to us for our own good.
Therefore you need to go ahead and live a
life of greatness.

Chapter Two

Faith

"Now faith is the substance of things hope for, the evidence of things not seen. (2). for by faith the elders obtained a better report. (3). through faith we understand that the worlds were framed by the word of God, so that things which are not seen were not made of things which do appear." Hebrew 11:1-3

For us to acquire massive wealth on this earth we need to have faith in God, in ourselves, and in any investment we getting into. The Bible has just made it clear to us that the things that we see today were not made by things that was seen but was framed by the word of God. I want you to understand that the grab of our blessings are placed within our reach by God when we step out in faith.

God respect, and reward anyone who works by faith. The scripture says in Hebrew 11:6 that, "But without faith it is impossible to please Him: for he that comes to God must believe that He is, and that He is a rewarded of them that diligently seek Him."

If you really need the blessings of massive wealth from God you need to go all out for Him by working in faith.

Thomas Edison's faith of persistence took through 10,000 experiments that failed before perfecting the incandescent light bulb; also the faith of persistence applied by Henry Ford gave him the success which he required from his engineers to create an engine with eight cylinders cast in one block. Even when his engineers said it is impossible for that to happen, Ford by faith instructed them to pursue his project anyway and remain on the job until they succeed, even after of voicing out of impossibility by his engineers, Ford's determination and faith to succeed suddenly made it happen. The famous V-8 engine became a reality. His unwavering faith revolutionized the automobile industry.

Today I want you to understand that if you have faith in God and faith in whatever you intend to do, with a strong desire without wavering you will have a successful result. Napoleon Hill once said in his book "Think & Grow." That, "whatever the mind of man can conceive and believe it can be achieved." Do you desire to go into business, or marriage, or lose weight, or go to school, or change a career? I am telling you today with a strong command that with the application of real faith you can turn your impossible dream to possibility need. Apply the 3 strategies below for quick success;

1. Focus on your imagination
2. Have a strong desire on what you need
3. Rightfully chose your associates or friends.

The Bible says that, "Let the Lord be magnified, which has pleasure in the prosperity of His servants," (Psalm 35:27)

our faith citrates us to an extra miles, it also

helps us to push a little harder to reach

higher.

Learning from the faith applied by 4

Lepers

And there were four leprous men at

the entering in of the gate: and they said, one

to another, why sit us here until we die? (4)

If we say, we will enter into the city, then

the famine is in the city, and we shall die

there: and if we sit still here, we die also.

Now therefore come, and let us fall unto the

host of the Syrians: if they save us alive, we

shall live; and if they kill us, we shall but die.

(5) And they rose up in the twilight, to go unto the camp of the Syrians: and when they were come to the uttermost part of the camp of the Syria, behold, there was no man there.

(6) For the Lord had made the host of the Syrians to hear a noise of chariots, and a noise of horses, even the noise of great host: and they said to one another, lo, the Kings of Israel hath hired against us the Kings of the Hittites, and the Kings of the Egyptians, to come upon us

SECTION II

THE POWER OF POSITIVE DESIRE

INTRODUCTION

Part two of this book is dedicated to T.L Osborn a great man of God whom I owe my respect to. Thought he is deceased but his impact for the kingdom of God still live fresh in me. He was one of the greatest and anointed Apostles of our time. He is one of my mentors and spiritual Father. His ministry has great impact in my life. I know this chapter will be a blessing to your life.

T.L Osborn is one of the most qualified people to be a part of this great book of life.

As long as this book exists his name will be heard and remembered.

About T.L Osborn (1923-2013)

Dr. T.L. Osborn was a world renounced missionary evangelist, teacher, author, statesman, publisher, linguist, designer, pianist, and administrator. This great man of God was known for his mass-miracle crusades to millions. With his wife & associate minister, Dr. Daisy Washburn Osborn, they established their headquarters in Tulsa, Oklahoma in 1949.

He met his wife, Daisy Washburn, when he was only 17, then she was 16. One year later they got married. At 20 and 21, they were missionaries in India. At 23 and 24, they had audiences from 10,000 to 25,000 who were coming to hear and listen to his teachings.

In his time he experienced over 53years of happiness, love, and international ministry together with his wife before she died in 1995.

T.L Osborn ministered in over 80 nations, and his audiences have numbered from 20,000 to 300,000 in stadiums, ball parks, race tracks, and out on open fields where people of all religions, creeds, and persuasions can freely attend.

He believes that the only authentic message from God is good news. So this section two will take us in-depth on his anointed revelation which he wrote in his book that will surely lead us to the way, and the truth in acquiring massive wealth.

Remember **Luke 1:37**

For with God nothing shall be impossible

CHAPTER THREE

LIBRATION FROM LIMITATION

According to **1Corinthians 2.9:10 Paul**

said that,

> **"But as it is written, Eye hath not**
>
> **seen, nor ear heard, neither have**
>
> **entered into the heart of man, the**
>
> **things which God hath prepared for**
>
> **them that love Him (9).**
>
> **But God hath revealed them unto**
>
> **us by His Spirit: for the Spirit**

searches all things, yea, and the

deep things of God (10)."

Here God is telling us every day.....

To desire the best,

To inquire of His way,

To admire His provisions,

To aspire to His blessings,

To require His abundance,

To acquire His lifestyle,

To inspire His posterity,

All this is because He loves us as His children. So it is ignorant for a child of God, who is created in the image of God to live under the bondage of mediocrity or poverty.

T.L. Osborn went further to elaborate that God our Father wants us to be liberated from all limitations imposed upon us by any person, condition or system because whoever God hath set free is free indeed. He said we don't need anybody's permission to be wealthy, healthy, happy and successful, for God has freed our wings of desire so that they can lift us to new frontiers and new fortunes.

He went further to elaborate that God's idea for us never changed, His idea is to share His life and His abilities with us, to make us happy, healthy, talented and prosperous. Jesus Christ summed it all in **John 10:10,**

…. I came that you might have life in abundance.

The only one that can stop us from having abundance (wealth) is us. If we don't believe this word by living in doubt we will never see the prosperity from God. So we need to believe in our heart that Jesus Christ is seated at the right hand of God today commanding us to go and take hold of our possessions, because He gave His life for us that we might live in abundance.

Psalm 84: 11 records that;

"For the Lord God is a sun and shield: the Lord will give grace and glory: no good thing will He withhold from them that walk uprightly."

Therefore you just need to believe that God who created you is your sun and shield that is why David in Psalm 121 says that, he look unto that hill from there come's his help. He went further to say that the Lord is his helper, the sun shall not smith him by day nor night, he also that the Lord shall preserve his going out and his coming in forever. Here David wants you to know that God is interested in your daily affairs, he wants you to prosper in all things. Already He has given us the grace which is the gift of God, the grace to make wealth without sweating. He is the One that glorifies with His abundance, what His need from us is just to act on faith. God is saying

to us every day....

1. My blessings makes rich and it adds

    no sorrow,

2. I am the One that gives you power to

    make wealth,

3. This is the set time to favor you

After reading and applying this book into

your life, you will have no more excuse not

to be wealthy. Whether you like it or not

the shower of abundance of wealth will

begin to flow in every area of your life

because every word written in this book has been proven with massive result.

Every material and spiritual possession acquired will come as a miracle (Grace) upon your life. Jesus Christ fed 5,000 men with nothing but they had enough and leftovers. A raven brought meat to Elijah when he was in the cave running away from Jezebel. The woman who obeyed the Prophet of God didn't run out of oil until she stopped bringing barrels. That God that did all that miracles by His Grace is the same God we have as Father today.

Just Believe!

The Unlimited Power of the Mind

The human mind has the unlimited power within to lift us up to greatness, our dreams and goals are determined by how we are able to effective used our mind. We just need to know how to control, and direct it to where it should go. According to Napoleon Hill, **"Whatever the mind of a man can conceive and believe it can achieve."** So this book will help you achieve your dreams by training you on how to use that unlimited power of the mind given to you by God.

The mind of a human composes of many qualities such as optimism and pessimism, hatred and love, kindness and cruelty, likes and dislikes, and more. The one you allow to dominate you easily showed up, therefore it is always advisable for one to live a lifestyle of storing in good words or good experiences.

Thoughts in our mind are like seed planted in the ground in that it produces a crop after its kind. With time it multiplies,

and grows; therefore, it is dangerous to
allow the mind to hold any thought which is
destructive. Such thoughts at the end are
been released through physical means which
is the result. Napoléon Hill said that
"through the principle of auto-suggestion-
that is, thoughts held in the mind and
concentrated upon, will soon begin to
crystallize into action." Therefore, the
human mind need the sunlight of
nourishment and use to keep them alive by
thinking positive at all time. Then the
only way to develop the mind is to
concentrate upon it, think about it, and use it
for good intentions. We can destroy any evil
tendency in our mind by not using it to think
negative.

The Bible said in Romans 12: 1-2,
"I beseech you therefore, brethren, by
the mercies of God, that ye present your
bodies a living sacrifice, holy, acceptable
unto God, which is your reasonable service.

And be not conformed to this world,
but are ye transformed by the renewing of
your mind, that ye may prove what is that
good, acceptable, and perfect, will of God."

What Paul is saying here is that for us to be of a good service in this generation our mind needs to be transformed. The question here is do you want to live a successful life on this earth? Then you need to be ready to renew your mind by feeding it daily with positive thinking that will prosper you, and the society. With strong confidence I want you to know that it is very possible for you to be rich in this world, and also live a peaceable life...

You need to understand that every thought which you store in your brain attracts elements after its kind, whether it is of destruction or construction, kindness or unkindness. It is also good to point out here that your human mind forms bonds only with other minds which are harmonious and have similar tendencies; therefore, the class of people which you attract depends upon the tendency of your own mind. You have the power to control those tendencies and can direct them along any line you choose, attracting to you any sort of person you wish. **2 Timothy 2:6-7 rightly stated that, "Wherefore I put thee in remembrance that thou stir up the gift of**

God, which is thee by the putting on of my hands.

For God hath not given us the spirit of fear; but of power, and of love, and of a sound mind." Paul here is encouraging Timothy to stir up the gift God in him because God has given him the power, love and sound mind. Therefore we need to guard our mind from fear of any sort because the devil may want to penetrate into our mind so that we will not be able to function in the area of our gifting's. Note hear that fear is one of the major hindrance to our prosperity.

How to Develop Our Mind

Since the developing qualities are largely determined by one's environment, associates, and training, and one's own thought, then it is very possible to be able to control our mind and achieve our goal through the following;

Firstly, if you really want to prosper in this life you need to use my **new method of invention for personal achievement known as "Science of Association."** This method proves that the

people you associate with have a part to play with what you store in your heart. The Bible said in **Proverbs 13:20 that,**
"He that walked with wise men shall be wise: but the companion of fools shall be destroyed." Wise men always bring wise words that will produce success. I am encouraging you to wisely choose your friends if you really want to make it in this life, friends and peer groups are those we see on daily bases, you can always agree with me that they come around us with their own daily experiences from their home, community, and even what they heard from the television or radio, the only place the can release all the information they store within is passing it across to us. Some information may be helpful but 80% of it can be destructive, so wisely choose your friends, and they should have a similar gifting. If your area of gifting is in business look for a mentor or friend in that area of profession, and should also be a successful business man. Make sure you are ready to humble yourself in a teachable spirit to learn, and to pay back your dues of retaliation knowing that nothing is free. What I meant is this, always be ready to give

back any thing as a reward to whomever that blesses you in any form of goodness.

Secondly is training, you need to rightly choose who you learn from , listen to, and the tapes you feed your mind with matters a lot if you really want develop your mind. The Bible said in **Philippians 4:8:9 that,**

"Finally, brethren, whatsoever things are true, whatsoever things are honest, whatsoever things are just, whatsoever things are pure, whatsoever things are lovely, whatsoever things are of good report; if there be any virtue, and if there be any praise, think on those things

Those things, which ye have both learned, and seen in me, do: and the God of peace shall be with you."

Brother Timothy in the Bible had Apostle Paul as his mentor, and that was who he learned from. Joshua in the Bible had Moses as his mentor that was why he became a good and power leader in Israel; Prophet Elisha had Prophet Elijah as his mentor that was why he became a strong and powerful Prophet; King David had Prophet Samuel who anointed him as a King because of this God was always with David. Every great leader who had ever existed had a mentor, just research it yourself.

Features of the Mind

The mind has features like any human; it has eyes, legs, body but operates like the spirit because of the unlimited power God placed in it. We have the power to control our mind by how we feed it with information, if the information store is healthy then our whole body and our affairs will be healthy, but if it is destructive then everything in us will be destructive. The Bible said in **Proverbs 4:23 that "Keep thy heart with all diligence; for out of it are the issues of life."**

Sometimes when you are alone, you can see that your mind travels to an unlimited distance and can even reflect the past feelings or experiences. If those experiences were bad it can affect the totally of your present and your future. Therefore you should be very quick to discern good or bad information immediately you hear someone starts speaking because good and wise words comes without persuading you to accept it, but the destructive words comes in a cunning form of persuasion and at times comes with much words for acceptance. You just need to guard your heart knowing that your success in this life lies in human good words you take in. I encourage guarding your mind by thinking and growing rich principle, which is by not allowing any negative words to come into your mind.

Secondly you need to commit your daily thought in prayer, and allow God in the name of Jesus Christ to direct your mind by His Spirit, **Romans 8:1 said that**,
"There is therefore no condemnation to them which are in Christ Jesus who walk not after the flesh but after the flesh, but after the Spirit."

Napoleon Hill 2 minute counseling for Achievers

The time and energy which we spend in striking back at those who anger us would make us independently wealthy if this great force were directed towards constructive effort- to building instead of tearing down!

It is the belief of Napoleon Hill that the average person spends three-fourths of his lifetime in useless, destructive effort. There is but one real way to punish a person who has wrong you, and that is by returning good for evil. The hottest coals ever heaped upon human being's head are acts of kindness in return for acts of cruelty.

Time spent in hatred not only is wasted, but it smothers the only worthwhile emotions of the human heart, and renders a person useless for constructive work. Thoughts of hatred do not harm anyone except the person indulges in them.

Whisky and morphine are no more deleterious to the human body than are thoughts of hatred and anger. Favor is the person who has grown to be big enough and wise enough to rise above intolerance, selfishness greed, and petty jealousies. These are the things which blot out the better impulses of the human soul and open the human heart to violence.

Great souls are usually housed in human beings who are slow at anger and who seldom try to destroy one of their fellowmen or defeat him in his undertakings.

The man or woman who can forgive and truly forget an injury by a fellow man is to be envied. Such souls rise to heights of happiness which most mortals never enjoy.

How long, oh God, how long will it be until human race will learn to walk down the pathway of life, helping one another in a spirit of love, instead of trying to cut one another down? How long will it be until we learn that the only real success in life is measured by the extent to which we serve humanity? How long will it be until we learn that life's richest blessings are bestowed upon the person who scorns to stoop to the vulgar attempt to destroy his fellow man?

The Way Forward

If the thing your store in your mind is right, and you truly believe in it, go ahead and put it in action and never give up when you meet any temporary defeat for there is always a seed an equivalent success in any failure.

Thomas Edison had in mind to invent a lamp that could be operated by electricity, began where he stood to put his dream into action, and history proves that despite more than ten thousand failures, he stood by that dream which he conceive in his mind until he made it a physical reality. It is good to know that practical dreamers who store good thoughts in their mind never quit!

The Wright brothers had in mind of a machine that would fly through the air. Now we see planes, helicopters and many more which is evidence all over the world that they dreamed soundly.

Marla Runyan is an American track and field athlete, road runner and marathon runner who are legally blind. By taking charged of her mind, feeding it with positive thinking she became a three time national champion in the women's 500 meters. Marla didn't allow being blind to stop her from achieving her goal in life. She took it off her mind and sees herself as a normal human being like everyone else. She sees with the eyes of a positive mind which urns to real faith. If a blind woman can make it in this life and become a champion, what do you say of yourself who has all the normal features as a human? I commend you to start dreaming and let only positive desire feel your mind.

SECTION III

DECISION TIME

CHAPTER FOUR
UNLEASHING YOUR UNLIMITED
HIDDEN POTENTIAL WITHIN YOU

1. You Have a Gift

The gift is in us, but we have the responsibility to stir it up. The apostle Paul wrote to Timothy, "For this reason I remind you to fan into flame the gift of God, which is in you" (2 Timothy 1:6).

In the New King James Version of the Bible, the verse is translated, "Stir up the gift of God," Which has the following features;

i.   The gift is not something we learn.
ii.   It is something God gave us.
iii.   It is something we need to discover and then stir up.
iv.   No one else can activate your gift for you.
v.   You have to do it yourself.

1. How do you stir up your gift?

Your gift can be stir up easily by developing, refining, enhancing, and using it. That's where education comes in.

Education can't give you your gift, but it can help you develop it so that it can be used to the maximum. Proverbs 17:8 says, "A gift is as a precious stone in the eyes of him that hath it: whithersoever it turned, it prosperity" (KJV). In other words, a gift is like a precious stone to the one who has it, when discovered and developed it turns into prosperity.

If your gift is put into used, it will prosper you. Many people today are working for money, that's an inferior reason to work. We must work for the vision within us.

Moreover, you are not to mimic the gifts of others, but rather stir up your own gift. Unfortunately, many people are jealous of other people's gifts, but let me encourage you not to waste your time on jealousy because jealousy is a gift robber; jealousy is an energy drain; jealousy will take away the passion of life from you. You should rather be busy stirring up your own gift, and then you won't have time to be jealous of anyone else or to feel sorry for yourself.

I sometime ago read an article about Louis Armstrong, the jazz artist, he reportedly applied to go to music school and was brought in for an audition. They gave him scales to sing, but he could sing only the first two notes properly, so they told him he didn't have what it takes to be a musician.

The story said that he cried because they rejected him from the music program. But Louis told his friends afterward, "I know there's music in me, and they can't keep it out." He eventually became one of the most successful and beloved jazz musicians. He sold more records and made more money than scores of others who were more talented at singing. Now he is forever etched in the history of music.

He said that though we are all born as originals, most of us become imitators. He went further to point out that he used to think about becoming like everyone else and joining the rat race. However, then I realized that if all the rats are in a race, and you win, you simply become the Big Rat.

I recommend that you get out of the rat race, stop competing with the community, stop being in a contest with society, stop trying to keep up with the Joneses, stop trying to please everybody, and say, "I'm not going to be a rat. I'm going to find my own niche.

I'm going to make room for myself in the world by using my gift."

2. Your gift makes room for you

"A man's gift makes room for him, and brings him before great men."
Proverbs 18:16

When God created us he placed in us

gifts and talents which are so unique that we

are different from any other person in this

planet earth. And that God given gift is able

to lift you to greater height in your area of endeavor. In course of life I discover that we all fall this victim of not valuing what we have but tends to run after what we don't or what we see people have. If we settle down and allocate or discover our gift which we play with every day without stress of any kind, then our ladder to success will be very easy.

What I meant is this; if your gift is to cook you make it well in life as a good Chef, feel happy, and also have this sense of accomplishment. There are people today that have made it in a certain area of profession but still not happy or do not find joy because they are in the wrong profession. Success is not defined on how much money or material wealth you acquire but doing what you can do best in ease and also find that peace in you which are that sense of accomplishment.

I have seen Billionaires commit suicide, and I have also seen celebrities commit suicide; live a miserable life of drugs, and substances all because they are doing what is not for them. You can always be in certain profession which is not your gift as a starting point because one needs to start from somewhere, for example, Tony

Robbins said 34years ago he had worked as a janitor before accomplishing what he is today as a billionaire. The emphasize here is that if you are in a certain profession that is not in your area of gifting, and you are successful, I will encourage you to spend much time to visualize, invest, nurture your proper gift because your joy and life span on earth will be determine by it. Other professions in your life will pass away but your gift will remain with you all through your life.

Know today that your gift will make room for you; it will recommend you;

introduce you, and always bring you to great men and women in this generation. The most important thing your gift will bring is peace of mind and sense of fulfilment.

3. Your gift is as precious stone to you

"A gift is as a precious stone in the eyes of him that hath it: whithersoever it turned, it prospered." Proverbs 17:8

You have to value your gift no matter how small it may look like. Just don't act like that man in the Bible which God gave him one gift and he was so angry because

God gave others more gift than him. Anger made him to bury his gift without using it.

Our God hate those who do not make use of their gift. Let your gift be as a precious stone in your eyes. You don't need any one to praise your gift other than you. Value, developed and always be bold to take risk with it because prosperity will come out of it.

Sometimes it takes time for us to see the fruit of our gift but as we wait patiently and continue to do we you do best, then the increase will begin to flow. The secret is that when it begins to produce results plus material wealth it do not stop, it fruit continues all through your life.

"Sees thou a man diligent in his business? He shall stand before Kings; he shall not stand before mean men."

Proverbs 22:29

When you are diligent in the area of your gifting great men and women will look for you. You don't need to run around looking for someone to recommend you. You just need to discover your gift and you will stand before Kings.

So be diligent (steady effort) in your gift for you will definitely stand out before Kings and Queens, people in this generation will honor and respect you. **Isaiah 60:15-17** rightly explains the blessings that will be inherited by someone that discover its God given gift.

"Whereas thou hast been forsaken and hated, so that no man went through thee. I will make thee an eternal Excellency, a joy of many generations.

Thou shalt also suck the milk of the Gentiles, and shalt suck the breast of Kings: and thou shalt know that I the

Lord am thy Savior and thy Redeemer, the Mighty One of Jacob.

For brass I will bring gold, and for iron I will bring silver, and for wood brass, and for stones iron: I will also make thy officers peace, and thine exactors' righteousness."

Here God is speaking through Prophet Isaiah to us that when we stay on the gift which He gave to us by the anointing of the Holy Spirit from creation then, we will find peace. He said we will be perfect; a blessing to many people in this our generation.

The Bible said in Romans 8:19 that,

"For the earnest expectation of the creature waited for the manifestation of the sons of God."

Here it is good to know that a lot of people are waiting to see you manifest your gift which is your hidden potential. They are expecting you to be blessing them with it. Then the question is what is holding you back? You need to put yourself now into action and begin to inherit the blessings of God upon your life. Begin to use your gift now, whatever you think brings peace and joy into your life. Philippians 4:8 says;

"Finally, brethren, whatsoever things are true, whatsoever things are honest, whatsoever things are just, whatsoever things are pure, whatsoever things are lovely, whatsoever things are of good report; if there be any virtue, and if there be any praise, think on these things."

4. Develop or stir up your Gift

"Wherefore I put thee in remembrance that thou stir up the gift of God which is in thee by the putting of my hands.

"For God hath not given us the spirit of fear; but of power, and of love, and of a sound mind." 2 Timothy 1:6

Paul was telling Brother Timothy not to be afraid to demonstrate the gifting of God upon his ministry. That he has the power and sound mind inside of him. So what I want you to learn is that you don't need to be afraid of any temporary setback in your life when you in the time of developing your gift. Setbacks will come but your strength is to learn from where you failed, and build success through it. Napoleon Hill in his book Said that, "Every adversity, every failure, heartache carries with it the seed on

an equal or greater benefit."

5. Everybody has a proper gift

"For I would, that all men were even as I myself. But every man hath his proper gift of God, one after this manner, and another after that."

Paul was explaining to the brethren that everyone has it proper gift from God. That your gift was being placed inside of you right from the day God created you and placed you inside your mother's womb. That gift has the dynamite to raise you up to any level of success in this planet earth.

Your gift is so valuable to God because He gave it to you as praise to Himself. He wants to glorify Himself through you so make good use of It., therefore whenever we make well of our gift on this earth, heaven rejoices.

Now it is your responsibility to develop your gift by continual putting it into practice. Your applied faith is able to overcome your fears because God had given you the spirit of sound mind. You only fall into worries when copy other people's gift, and neglect your own proper gift from God.

Therefore your gift makes you original, and

gives us that confidence that you know what

you are doing. Then stand by your gift,

make sure you respect, develop and work

with it for prosperity will be your friend.

6. God gives the gift

"Every good gift and every perfect gift

is from above, and cometh down from the

Father of lights, with who is no

variableness, neither shadow of turning."

James 1:17

The shortcut to discovering your hidden potential which is the gift of God upon your life is to get connect with Him at all time. As you can see in this passage of the Bible there are good and perfect gift, which means there are as bad and imperfect gift. Here it is very easy differentiate them in case of rightful judgment, God and Satan is involved, the perfect gift is from God used for the good of this generation, while the bad gift is from Satan used to do evil. It is very easy to discern a good gift from a bad gift.

My point here is that when God creates a human, He placed inside of him a gift which by His grace. The gift is an unmerited favor to all humans, the purpose of the gift is for us to be able to succeed and live peaceably in this generation. It is very possible for you to acquire massive wealth, and also live an affluent life in this generation if only you can connect with God by giving Him your quite time. He will reveal your gift to you and His gift is without repentance, when He gives us a thing He do not take it back, that is why He is a good God, and also a Father to us.

Something to think about

God's gift upon your life is to help you to inherit the blessings of Psalm 8

1. To still the enemy and the avenger

2. As a remembrance that you are a child of God, and that He visit's you always

3. That you are a little lower than the Angels

4. It is also a prove that you are crowned with glory and honor

5. It will also help you to have dominion over the work God has entrusted into your hand

6. God hast put all things under your

   feet through the gift He gave to you

SECTION IV

SUCCESSFUL PEOPLE THAT USED THEIR GIFT TO ACHIEVE GREATNESS

CHAPTER FIVE

EXAMPLES OF SUCCESSFUL PEOPLE

1. King David

"Then Samuel took the horn of oil, and anointed him in the midst of his brethren: and the Spirit of the Lord came upon David from that day forward. So Samuel rose up, and went to Ra-mah.

But the Spirit of the Lord departed from Saul, and an evil spirit from God troubled him.

And Saul's servants said unto him, Behold now, an evil spirit from God troubled thee.

Let our lord now command thy servants, which are before thee, to seek out a man, who is a cunning player on a harp: and it shall come to pass, when the evil spirit from God is upon thee, that he shall play with his hand, and thou shall be well.

And Saul said unto his servants, provide me now a man that can play well, and bring him to me.

Then answered one of the servants, and said, Behold, I have seen a son of Jesse the Bethlemite that is cunning in playing, and a mighty valiant man, and a man of war, and a prudent in matters, and is comely person, and the Lord is with him.

Wherefore Saul sent messengers unto Jesse, and said, send me David thy son, which is with the sheep." 1 Samuel 16:13-19

David was a boy who was always in the field taking care of his father's sheep, and one remarkable gift he had was playing of musical instrument called harp. He discovered that this is what he loved and chooses to play it as a daily practice for fun. As we read in the chapter above, it was this gift of playing cunning instrument that took him to the palace to play for the King.

As we earlier understood that a man that is diligent in his business will stand before Kings. David stood before King Saul because he was diligent in his business by perfecting his playing of the cunning instrument. We also learned in our previous chapter that the gift of a man will make room for him, and it prospers wherever he turns. Here David's gift made room for him in the palace with King Saul

What I am putting across here is that when you discover your gift, put it action through practicing, you will surely have favor in all your doings.

2. Joseph's Gift of interpretations of dreams

"And it came to pass at the end of two full years that Pharaoh

dreamed: and, behold, he stood by the river.

And behold, there came up out of the river seven well favored kine and fat fleshed; and they fed in a meadow.

And, behold, seven other kine came up after them out up after them out of the river, ill-favored and lean fleshed; and stood by the other kine upon the brink of the river.

And the ill-favored and lean fleshed kine did eat up the seven well favored and fat kine. So Pharaoh awoke.

And he slept and dreamed the second time: and behold, seven ears of corn came up upon one stalk rank and good.

And behold seven thin ears and blasted with the east wind sprung up after them.

And the seven thin ears devoured the seven rank and full ears. And Pharaoh woke, and behold, it was a dream.

And it came to pass in the morning that his spirit was troubled; and sent and called for all the magicians of Egypt, and all the wise men thereof: but there was none that could interpret them unto pharaoh.

Then spoke the chief butler unto pharaoh, saying, I do remember my faults this day:

Pharaoh was wroth with his servants, and put me in ward in the captain of the guard's house, both me and the chief baker:

And we dreamed a dream in one night, I and he; we dreamed each man according to the interpretation of his dream.

And there was there with us a young man, a Hebrew, servant to the captain of the guard; and we told him, and he interpreted to us our dreams; to each man according to his dream he did interpret.

And it came to pass, as he interpreted to us, so it was; me he restored unto mine office, and him he hanged.

Then Pharaoh sent and called Joseph, and they brought him hastily out of the dungeon: and he shaved himself, and changed his raiment, and came in unto Pharaoh." Genesis 41: 1-14

The point here is that Joseph's gift gave him the open door to meet Pharaoh who is the king of Egypt. Even while there in the prison the Chief Butler confirms that Joseph was exercising his gift of interpretation dreams. So no matter how your gift may look like, or no matter where you are declaring your gift it doesn't matter, because one day it will prosper you anyhow. His gift took from the prison to the palace where he was made the prime minister in charge of food which made the second in command to Pharaoh.

Your God given gift is all that you
need to survive in this generation, so
whatever it will take for you to discover it; I
encourage you to spend all that you have for
it. Discovering your gift is similar to finding
a good wife, which is a favor from God.

SECTION V

THE POWER OF IMAGINATION

CHAPTER SIX

THE MASTER KEY OF THE POWER OF

IMAGINATION

"And the Lord said, Behold, the people is one, and they have all one language; and this they begin to do: And now nothing will be restrained from them, which they have imagined to do." Genesis 11:6

Your Imagination is an invisible key in your mind that has the capability to unlock the incredible potential of your prosperity.

The two major functions of your mind are your memory and Imagination; both of them are the wonderful gift given to us by God. They can either raise you up to a greater height or hurt you.

The memory part helps us to see the pictures of our past, while our Imagination on the other hand creates and replays pictures of things we want to happen in our future.

For example, God told Abraham in Genesis 13:14-15 I quote,

"And the Lord said to unto Abram, after that Lot was separated from him, Lift up now thine eyes, and look from the place where thou art northward, and southward, and eastward, and westward:

For all the land which thou sees, to thee will I give it, and to thy seed forever.

And I will make thy seed as the dust of the earth: so that if a man can number the dust of the earth, then shall thy seed also be numbered.

Arise; walk through the land in the length of it and in the breath of it; for I will give unto thee."

God in this chapter expected Abraham to use his imagination to picture his future, and the future of Israel.

I want you to understand that Abraham's imagination strengthened his faith. And through the power imagination Isaac which was the promise of God was conceived in old age.

Another good example of the power of imagination was when David had to fight

Goliath. The Bible said that Goliath was a great man of war, a champion of the Philistines, with multiple years of experience, always ready to fight and win. Goliath profile history is something to think about before engaging him for a fight. David with no outstanding military experience decided to fight him, but the only way he could encourage himself is to mentally playback his previous victories of when he killed bear and lion as he was taking care of his father's sheep in the field. Then with his imagination he pictured and replayed his impending victory over Goliath.

Hear what David said when he was
about to fight Goliath 1Samuel 18:45-47, 50

"Then said David to the Philistine, thou
come to me with a sword, and with a spear,
and with a shield: but I come to thee in the
name of the Lord of hosts, the God of the
armies of Israel, whom thou hast defied.

This day will the Lord deliver thee
into mine hand; and I will smite thee, and
take thine head from thee; and I will give
the carcasses of the host of the Philistines
this day unto the fowls of the air, and to the

wild beasts of the earth; that all the earth

may know that there is a God in Israel.

And all this assembly shall know that

the Lord saved not with sword and spear:

for the battle are the Lord's and He will give

you into our hands.

Verse 50, David prevailed over the

Philistine with a sling and with a stone, and

smote the Philistine, and slew him; but

there was no sword in the hand of David."

Therefore, I encourage you to use

your God given inspired imagination to

think of ways in which you can harness your

handicap, make profit from your problem,

capitalize on your crisis, and perhaps even

make your situation serve you.

How to Make Your Imagination Release

Your prosperity;

1. Choose a goal. Achievers are people

   who have this strong believe in

   setting goals for personal

   achievement. They also know that

   nothing is impossible they stop

   setting goals. Therefore I will

   encourage to make up your mind that

   goal-setting is absolutely necessary

for if actual need to be successful in

this life. An Austrian psychiatrist once

said that, "Goals give meaning to

living." Therefore, goals are very

much essential to us because they

motivate, and keep us alive.

According to Dr. Robert Schuller he

tells us that, "Not having a goal is

more to be feared than not reaching

a goal."

2. Use your imaginative power to think

   out possible ways to reach at your

   goal.

3. Make sure you excommunicate every temporary setback of fear from your imagination. This can be achieved by creating positive goal in your mind by disciplining your daily thinking, prohibiting that goal killer called fear from making entrance into the sacred cathedral of your God-given mind. Robert Browning once said that, "A man's reach should exceed his grasp, or what a heaven is for?" James Rusell Lowell also said, "Not failure, but low aim, is crime."

I will sum up here with Dr. Robert Schuller saying, "I would rather attempt to do something great and fail, than attempt to do nothing and succeed!"

4. Take action by getting started. Begin by writing down your ideas in paper. Put down a detailed outline on how you want to around what you want to setup. According to J.C. Penny he said, "The hardest part of any job is getting started." I want you to understand that big things started

with small positive ideas. Just give

your dream a start for you will

achieve it.

5. Imagine, and setup big goals beyond

your goals. Henry Ford setup a goal

which looked so impossible in the

eyes of all his engineers but because

he stood by it and made sure fear

never penetrates into his mind. He

accomplished what he wanted.

He is not different from you

because you can also achieve

whatever you want if only your can

dream big and follow after it.

SECTION VI

THE MASTER KEY OF SEED-FAITH

CHAPTER SEVEN

THE MASTER KEY OF SEED-FAITH

The power of giving is the secret of an abundant life. The lifestyle of giving is the weapon used to break the backbone of poverty in your life. For example,

1. Give to the poor

Proverbs 19:17 says that, "He that hath pity upon the poor lends unto the Lord; and that which he hath given will he pay him again."

Also Proverbs 28:27 says that, "He that gives unto the poor shall not lack: but he that hides his eyes shall have many a curse."

Therefore if you really want to prosper in and easy way, just have the poor at heart. As you give, God blesses.

2. Give to the ministers of God.

1 Kings 17:15-16 says that, "And she went and did according to the saying of Elijah: and she, and he, and her house, did eat many days.

And the barrel of meal wasted not, neither did the cruse of oil fail, according to the word of the Lord, which He spoke by Elijah."

The Bible verses above states that the Zarephath woman had her last meal to eat with her child before she die, but when she gave some to Prophet Elijah, record shows that God in turn blesses her with plenty that sustains her and her child. So when we give to the men and women of God there is this assurance that God will give back to you in abundance.

Jesus Christ said in Matthew 10:41-42

that, "He that receives a Prophet in the

name of a Prophet shall receive a Prophet's

reward; and he that receives a righteous

man in the name of a righteous man shall

receive a righteous man's reward.

And whosoever shall give to drink

unto one of these little ones a cup of cold

water only in the name of a disciple, verily I

say unto, he shall in no wise lose his

reward."

3. Giving to the work of God.

Jesus Christ said in Luke 6:38 that,

"Give, it shall be given unto you; good

measure, pressed down, and shaken

together, and running over, shall men give

into your bosom. For with the same

measure that ye mete withal it shall be

measured to you again."

Solomon also wrote in Proverbs 3:9-

10 that, "Honor the Lord with thy

substance, and with the first fruits of all

thine increase:

So shall thy barns be filled with

plenty, and thy presses shall burst out with

new wine."

In summary

1. A Seed is anything you can

   contribute to another.

2. Seed-Faith is when you plant your

   seed with an expectation of a

   specific harvest.

3. When you give an offering to God,

   your time, your skill, your energy,

   your labor. These are all important

to God which makes Him act on

your behave.

4. To God your money represents

you

AUTHORS CLOSING STATEMENT

Galatians 6:9

"And let us not be weary in well doing: for in due season we shall reap, if we faint not."

Think and grow rich! For Napoleon Hill once said in his book that "Whatever the mind of man can conceive and believe it can achieve."

Jesus Christ the King of Kings also said in Matthew 21:22 that, "And all things, whatsoever ye shall ask in prayer, believing,

ye shall receive."

Made in the USA
Coppell, TX
21 October 2021